NOTEPAD

INW

IDEALNEWWORLD.COM